# The Changing Face of Urchfont

## A Pictorial Record of the Parish

Published in 2005 by Urchfont Parish Trust
Layout and typesetting by Peter Greed, Margaret Clough,
Richard and Janet Hawkins
Cover designed by Peter Greed
Printed by Cromwell Press Ltd, Trowbridge

Copyright 2005 Urchfont Parish Trust
Urchfont Post Office
The Green
Urchfont
Devizes
Wilts
SN10 4QU

ISBN 0-9540851-1-6

**Project Group**
Elaine Bancroft
Margaret Clough
Christine Dolan
Peter Greed
Peter Newell
Peter Thorpe (until October 2003)
with the assistance of
Pam Cooke and Terry Dutton for Wedhampton

Proof Reader – Janet Hawkins

Publication of this book has been made possible by income from the sale of
*Urchfont by any other name,* a history of the Parish

# CONTENTS

Introduction

The Parish of Urchfont – Parish map
Urchfont – Street map
       – Duke of Queensberry map 1784
       – Watson-Taylor Estate map 1832
Aerial Views of Urchfont
Townsend
Ballingers and Stonepit Lane
Urchfont Manor, Newsyde and Goosehole
The Green and Blackboard Lane
Cuckoo Corner and Crookwood Lane
Peppercombe and Church Lane
St Michael and All Angels Church
The Pond Area
High Street
The Bottom
Uphill
Foxley and Crooks Lane
Lydeway
Wedhampton – Street map
       – Watson-Taylor Estate map 1832
Wedhampton
Green Gate Road
The Cartway
High Street
Plum Lane

# INTRODUCTION

This book came about as a direct result of the work undertaken on production of the earlier Urchfont Parish history – *Urchfont by any other name*. A large number of photographs came to hand which could not be accommodated and it was thought essential that an opportunity should be found to publish a significant proportion of this invaluable historical archive.

The prime purpose of this publication is to provide a photographic record of the Parish including Wedhampton and Lydeway. The Project Group have sifted and collated hundreds of photographs into a manageable publication and modern photographs have been included to illustrate some of the significant changes. For reasons of space, it has not been possible to provide as much information on individual properties as one would wish but some fuller information is available in *Urchfont by any other name*. Whilst every effort has been made to attribute a date or approximate date to the pictures wherever feasible, the Project Group have not resorted to mere guesswork.

The Project Group are indebted to all those who offered the use of their family photographs. They are particularly grateful to Skyviews Aerial Archives, the Campaign to Protect Rural England (CPRE), Mrs Maureen Woolfall, Richard Hale, Urchfont Women's Institute, Richard Hawkins, Elaine and Paul Bancroft, Peter Greed, the Wiltshire Buildings Record and Wiltshire County Council's Libraries and Heritage Department for permission to reproduce photographs for which they hold the copyright. The Project Group have endeavoured to obtain permission where necessary to reproduce photographs for which copyright may be held by others. They would be pleased to be advised should there be instances where any copyright may have been breached.

The Project Group hope that this publication will provide pleasure and happy memories for all those with a love for the Parish, past and present residents and visitors to the Parish.

Peter Newell
Chairman, Project Group 2005

# The Parish of URCHFONT – Parish map

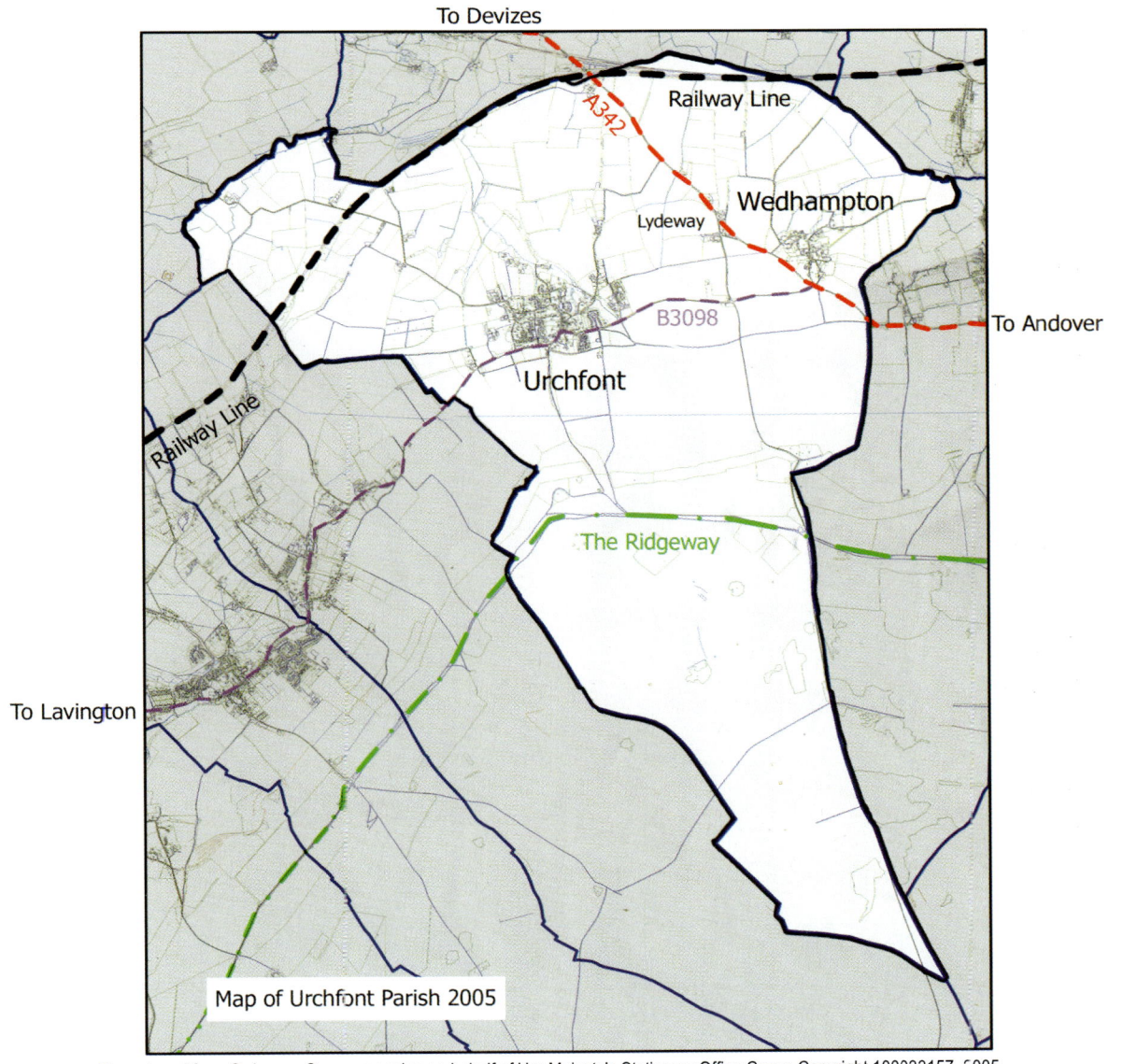

# URCHFONT – Street map

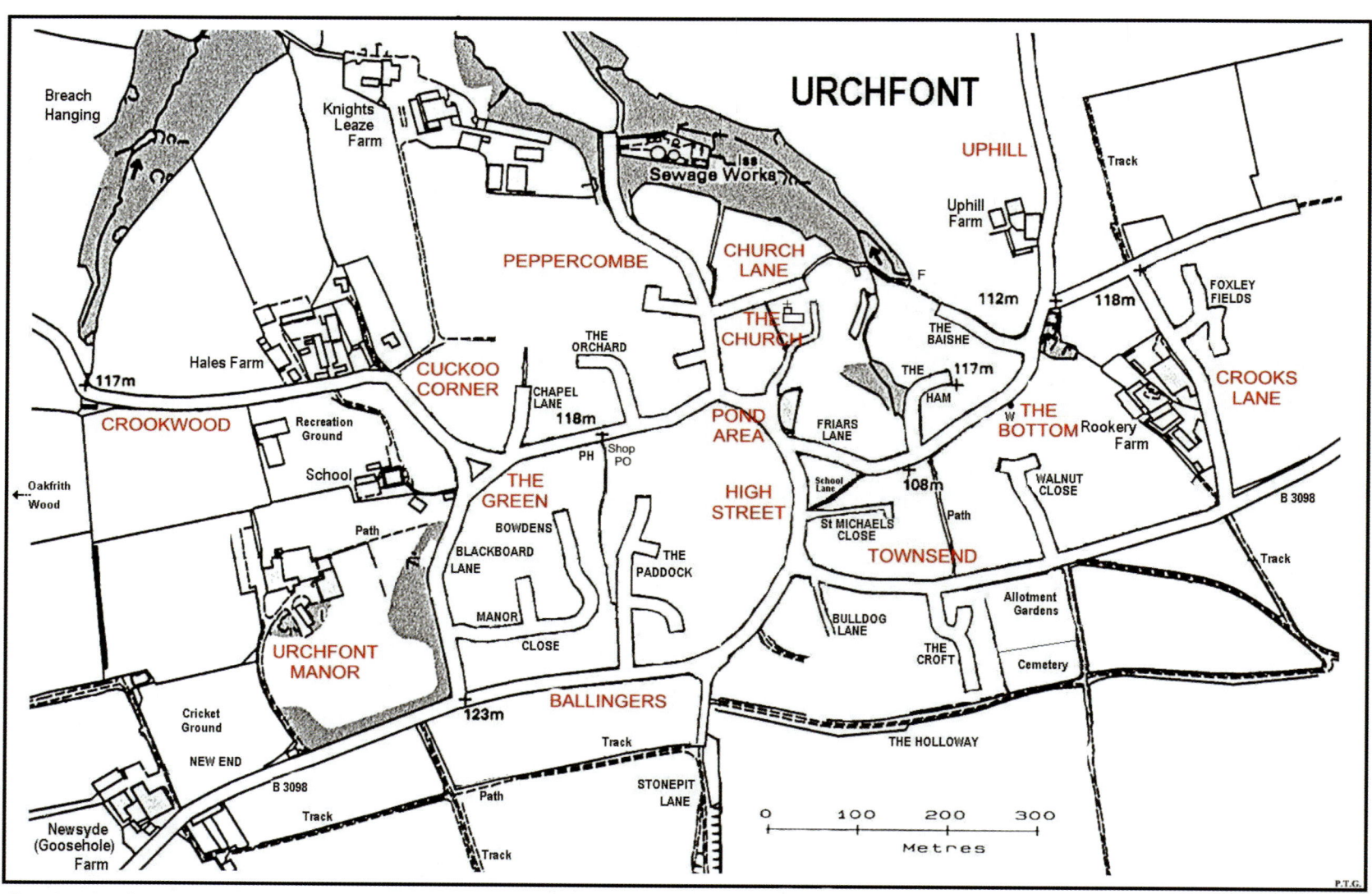

# URCHFONT – Duke of Queensberry map 1784

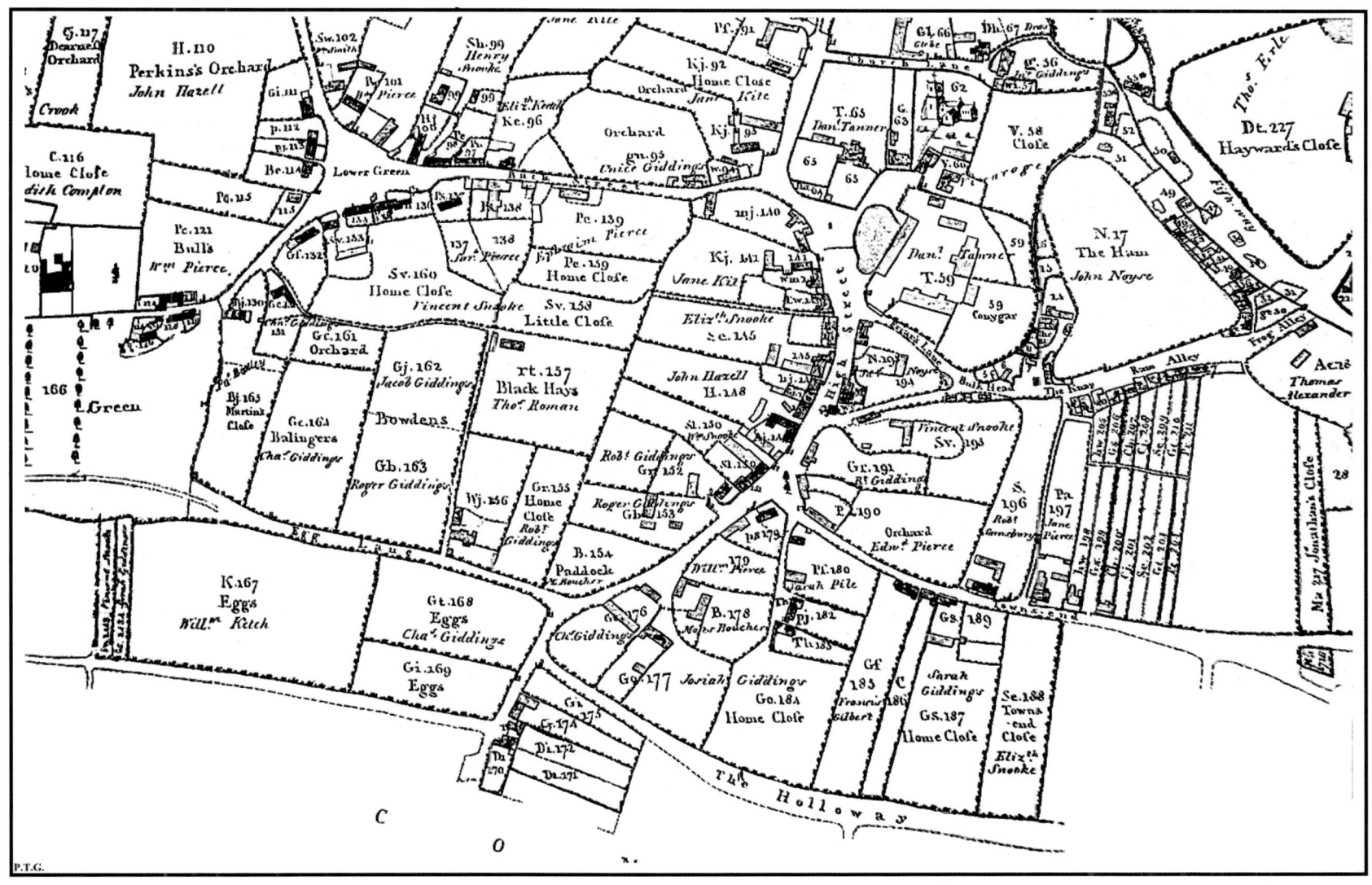

# URCHFONT – Watson-Taylor Estate map 1832

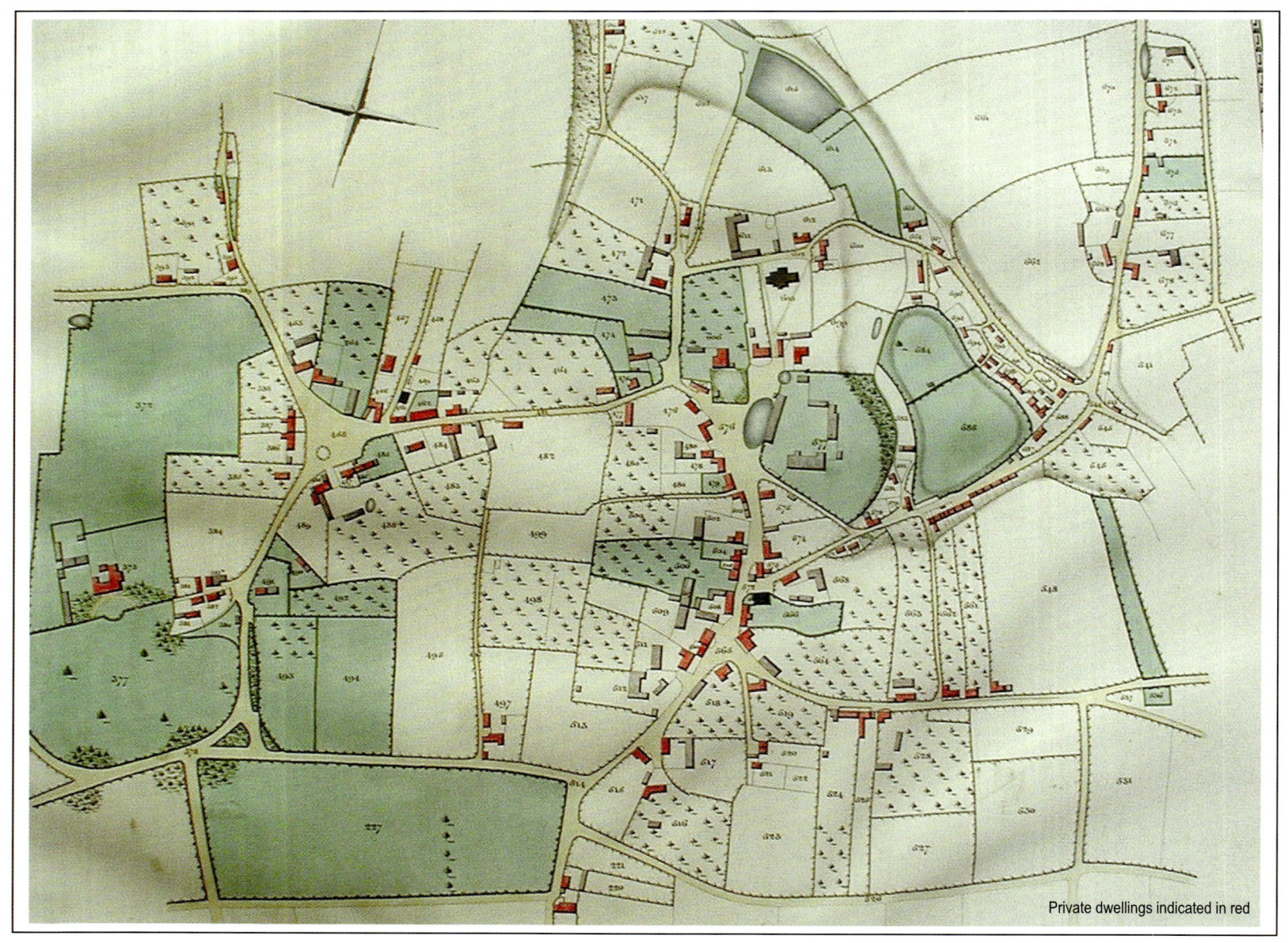

Private dwellings indicated in red

# AERIAL VIEWS OF URCHFONT

**URCHFONT VILLAGE** 1984.   Looking from the north (bottom of the picture) up to the south (Townsend on the left and Ballingers and Blackboard Lane top right).   *(Courtesy Richard Hale)*

# AERIALS URCHFONT

**URCHFONT VILLAGE** *2000*

**Left:** *A view looking north with the Church in the centre towards the top of the picture and The Croft bottom right*

**Right:** *A view looking north east towards Uphill at the top of the picture with, further down to the right, Walnut Close. The Orchard can be seen on the left, towards the bottom of the picture, and The Paddock and Bowdens in the centre.*

**Four views of the village from the Church Tower**  AERIALS URCHFONT

*1920, showing the rear of **Mulberry House** in the foreground, **Manor Farmyard** (including the old tithe barn, demolished by fire in the 1950s), High Street, and Urchfont Hill at the top*

*Post-1920, slightly more to the west with the great cedar in the centre*

*2004, looking south east with the **Old Vicarage** in the foreground and **Manor Farmyard** to the rear*

*2004, looking south west, after the great cedar fell down in January 2003*

# AERIALS URCHFONT

**URCHFONT VILLAGE** *2000. Three long views of the village looking north from Salisbury Plain, from west (top) to east (bottom).*

# Townsend

The roadway leading east from the village towards Lydeway has been known as Townsend since at least the early 17th century, but the area has changed in recent times with the disappearance of two small farms and the development of new housing at Walnut Close and The Croft and some modern infilling along the north side of the road.

*An aerial view of* **URCHFONT** *with* **Townsend** *in the foreground, probably mid-20th century*

# TOWNSEND

*An aerial view 2001, with **Walnut Close** to the right and **The Croft** and the allotments at the bottom of the picture*

**Cemetery Gateway** 2004

**The Bier House** and **Cemetery** 2004

**Bus Shelter** erected in 2003

# TOWNSEND

**Left: Veranda House** and **Walnut House**
Early 20th century. This picture must have been taken from the bank opposite Veranda House (on the left), the road in between being hidden below the vegetation on the bank. Walnut House, in the centre of the picture, was at one time the farmhouse of Walnut Farm, a small area of land to the east now developed as Walnut Close. The thatched cottage shown in the picture to the right of Walnut House was demolished.

**Below Left:** Another picture of **Walnut House** (centre), probably taken about the same time from the opposite angle, with part of **Veranda House** to the left and the thatched cottage to the right

**Walnut House**, a view taken in 2004

**Right:** Another view of ***Veranda House*** and ***Walnut House*** from a lower angle, with a rather blurred view of the thatched cottage, now demolished, to the far right. Early 20th century.

**Left:** ***Veranda House*** taken in 2004 from the same angle as the earlier picture above

# TOWNSEND

*Left:* **Redhone Cottage** is almost unrecognisable in this early picture taken c1900. **Croft Cottage**, then thatched, is to the left of Redhone Cottage. To the left of the picture is **Townsend Farm** which was demolished in the late 1960s and the site, with some orchard ground to the east on which poultry were formerly kept, was redeveloped as **The Croft**.

*Right:* A modern view of **Redhone Cottage**, taken in 2002, with **Croft Cottage** to the left

**TOWNSEND.** *Aerial view taken in April 1966, with* **Townsend Cottages** *on the right,* **The Bungalow** *on the left and, in the foreground, the backs of* **Redhone Cottage**, **Croft Cottage** *and the former* **Townsend Farm**. *At the top of the picture are* **1** *and* **2** **St Michael's Close**.

*(Courtesy Skyviews Aerial Archives)*

# TOWNSEND

**Above: Townsend Cottage** at the end of a row of cottages, generally known as **Townsend Cottages**, is believed to be of 17th or 18th century origin. The end gable of Townsend Cottage incorporates an earlier cruck beam which is all that remains of a 15th or 16th century cottage next door. Since this picture was taken (1975) Townsend Cottage has been renovated, but the cruck beam is still clearly visible. *(Courtesy WI)*

**Above:** *A view of the whole row of* **Townsend Cottages**, *1975*
*(Courtesy WI)*

**Right: Townsend Cottages** *in 2004*

**Above: Bulldog Cottage** 1975
*(Courtesy WI)*

**Above: Bulldog Cottage**
*from the rear 2004*

**Bulldog Lane Cottages** 2004

# TOWNSEND

*Right: **The Rockeries** and **Hillsborough** c1900. The house now called **The Rockeries** was built in 1892 as the home and business premises of the saddler, Harry Fuller (shown standing at the front of the shop to the right of the picture; his wife, Ann, is sitting under the lamp). In the 1920s the business was moved to shop premises over the road and The Rockeries became a private house and bay windows were added at the front. The beautiful iron railings went for scrap during the Second World War. **Hillsborough** is to the left of the picture.*

*Left: **The Rockeries** and **Hillsborough** in 2002*

# BALLINGERS AND STONEPIT LANE

The part of the B3098, which runs to the south of the village eastwards from Blackboard Lane to its junction with High Street, was named Ballingers after a field in the area in the 18th century. It was formerly known as Egg Lane, by which name it appears in the Duke of Queensberry map of 1784. Stonepit Lane has long been a well-defined track onto the Plain. At one time sand and stone were excavated from the hollow area to the south of the village.

**BALLINGERS** and **STONEPIT LANE Houses** 2005. The row of eight semi-detached council houses numbered **1 to 8 Ballingers** to the left of the picture were built soon after the First World War to meet a need for affordable homes after a number of older dwellings in the village had been demolished. In the centre of this picture are **1 & 2 Haggs Lane** and to the right some later council-built houses **9 to 14 Stonepit Lane**.

# BALLINGERS

**Left: Highfield, BALLINGERS** 2004. This was the first bungalow to be built in Urchfont and was built in 1924. This picture shows Doris Lanfear in her garden.

**Right: 9–14 STONEPIT LANE** 2004. These six council houses were built during the Second World War at the bottom of Stonepit Lane. Curiously, they are numbered 9 to 14 (following on from the Ballingers numbering) even though their address is Stonepit Lane.

*Right:* **Stonepit Farm** *early 20th century. The farmhouse and farm buildings were quite close to the village a few hundred yards up Stonepit Lane on the left-hand (eastern) side. It was a working farm until the early part of the 20th century when the farmhouse roof was blown off in a storm and the farmhouse and other buildings were later demolished.*

*Left:* **STONEPIT LANE** *early 20th century showing* **Stonepit Farm** *and, to the right of the picture, the sand and stone excavation site. The sand was used in the cement for building the Village Hall in 1929.*

**Left: Urchfont Hill Farm** c1900. The farmhouse and buildings were at the top end of Stonepit Lane on the Plain. After the War Department acquired the land on the Plain in the early part of the 20th century, the farmhouse had to be evacuated during firing practice although farming continued until the late 1920s. The buildings were demolished in the mid-20th century.

**Right: Urchfont Hill Farm Cottage** c1900

# Urchfont Manor, Newsyde and Goosehole

Lying to the west of the village, this area was part of the original Upper Green and, further west, Workforth Common. Until 1947 all the properties in the area were part of the former Urchfont Manor Estate.

**Urchfont Manor** *1999, west elevation*

# THE MANOR

**Urchfont Manor** *c1920/30, east (front) and south elevation. The Manor, built c1680 for Sir William Pynsent, was purchased by Wiltshire County Council in 1946 for use as an Adult Education Residential College.* *(Courtesy CPRE)*

**Urchfont Manor** *c1922, east front*
*(Courtesy CPRE)*

**Urchfont Manor**, *west elevation*
*(now front access)*

# THE MANOR

**Left: Urchfont Manor Grounds** view across to **Fidler's Cottage** and **The Ark** on the left and **The Rank Cottages** in Back Street (The Green) centre right. **Fosbury Cottage** is to the far right of the picture.

**Below: Urchfont Manor Home Farm** c1930, now converted into seminar rooms and offices  (Courtesy CPRE)

**Above: Urchfont Manor Lodge** 2004

# THE MANOR

*Left:* **Old Wickham Green Farmhouse**, Witchell Lane 1954. Part of the Urchfont Manor Estate until 1947 when it was sold at auction by the Executors and Trustees of the will of Hamilton Rivers-Pollock. It was demolished in the late 1950s.

*Above:* **Witchell Cottage** prior to extension. A late 19th century cottage, it was also part of the Urchfont Manor Estate and sold at auction in 1947.

*Right:* **Witchell House** 2004, showing original cottage on left with subsequent extensions built in 1974 and 1985

*Below:* **The Shieling, Downlands** and **The Cottage**, New End 2004, were also part of the Urchfont Manor Estate until 1947

*Left:* **Goosehole Farmhouse** 2004, formerly Newsyde (the home of Fred Self, Farmer) and, before that, called New End Farmhouse. It was auctioned as part of the Urchfont Manor Estate in 1947.

# The Green and Blackboard Lane

The triangular green towards the western end of the village, strictly 'The Green' but sometimes called 'The Top Green', forms part of a much wider area designated The Green for postal purposes. It includes what was once called Back Street running from High Street up to the triangular green and from there to Blackboard Lane to the south and Cuckoo Corner to the north.

**THE GREEN (south side)** c1950 viewed from **Green Farm**, with children dancing round the maypole. **Burwood**, **Little Burwood** and **West End Farm** are in the background

# THE GREEN

*Above:* **THE GREEN (south side)** *early 20th century, with from left to right,* **Shepherds Cottage, No. 1 The Green, Burwood, Little Burwood** *and* **West End Farm**

*Left:* Detail of **Burwood** 1975 showing the timber framing which indicates that this house, probably of 17th century origin, was once a single storey building. Later, extra timber was added and the roof raised.
(Courtesy WI)

*Above:* A closer view of **No. 1 The Green**, **Burwood** and **Little Burwood** (in those days a paraffin shop). Early 20th century.

*Left:* **THE GREEN (south side)** 2004 showing, from right to left, **Little Burwood, Burwood, No. 1 The Green, Shepherds Cottage** and a glimpse of **Cameron Mo**, built in 1983, on the far left

THE GREEN

***Above:*** **West End Farm** *as it was in the early 20th century. Originally a single storey building, West End Farm is thought to have been built in the late 16th or early 17th century.*

***Below:*** *Two modern views taken in 2004 of* **West End Farm** *(on the left) and its barn (on the right). The barn, which stands at the rear of West End Farm, has the date 1751 on its timbers and incorporates the remains of an earlier cob building and fireplace.*

# THE GREEN

*Right: **Rose Cottage** pre-1928. The cottage in this photograph has been so altered over the years that it bears very little resemblance to the present day **Fosbury Cottage**, but the thatched roof of West End Farm, clearly visible at the rear of the cottage, confirms its identity. The cottage was later named Pooles after the name of the field over the road on the Manor estate, sometimes called Bull's (so-named in the Queensberry map) before being named Fosbury Cottage in the mid-20th century. (The light-coloured area to the right of the picture is the roof of a shed at the back of West End Farm.)*

*Left: **Fosbury Cottage** in 2004. The corner of West End Farm roof can just be seen above the roofline*

# THE GREEN

**Left: Rosings** 1975. This cottage was formerly known as 'Ferris Cottage' (after Tink Ferris who once lived there). It is tucked away on the left of The Green running up to Blackboard Lane. *(Courtesy WI)*

**Below: Rosings** in 2004, showing the more recent white timbered extension at the rear

**Above:** *The barn behind Rosings 1975* *(Courtesy WI)*

**Right: Threeways, Blackboard Lane** 2004 has been the home of Felix and Phyllis Harris since its construction in 1948 on what was formerly a small woodland area of larches

# THE GREEN

**Left: THE GREEN (west side)** showing, from the right, **Oakfrith Cottage**, **Manor Cottage** and **The Ark** (all of late 17th or early 18th century origin) and a glimpse of the long sloping roof of **Fidler's Cottage**. This photograph was probably taken in the mid-20th century, possibly at the time of the Coronation judging by the Union Jack flying near the doorway of Manor Cottage and what appears to be bunting on The Ark.

**Right: Fidler's Cottage** 2004. This 18th century cottage (now a residential unit of Urchfont Manor) was formerly known as 'The Hencoop' or 'Violet Cottage'. For a time during the early part of the 20th century it was the village police station.

**Right: Fidler's Cottage** side view, 2004 showing the steeply sloping roof covering the back extension

# THE GREEN

**Right: The Ark** taken in 1927, with Miss Joan Denmark (later Mrs Michael Ferris) and one of the two Crocker sisters from next door Manor Cottage. The Crocker girls were reputed to be the prettiest girls in Urchfont at the time! The Ark is of late 17th or early 18th century origin with a top storey added towards the end of the 19th century. At one time the house was called 'Green House', but when, or why, the name was changed is not known.

**Above:** Side view of **The Ark** 2004. This picture shows where the extra storey was added.

**Right: THE GREEN (west side)** in the snow, December 1999

# THE GREEN

*Above:* **THE GREEN (north side)**. This photograph was taken in 1930 and shows **Oakfrith Cottage** on the left, **Pynsent Cottage** and **Green Farm** on the right, all thought to be of 17th century origin. Pynsent Cottage was once two cottages, one of which was the home of the Urchfont Manor blacksmith. His smithy was in a barn at the rear of the cottages, fronting the road, now converted into a bedroom. Green Farm was refaced in brick in the 18th century.

*Below:* **Oakfrith Cottage** *April 1989 on fire after a passing hay wagon damaged an overhead electricity cable causing a spark which set light to the thatched roof*

THE GREEN

**Left: Pynsent Cottage** c1960. Firemen pose in front of the cottage after putting out a fire which had destroyed the roof.

**Below: Green Farm** in 2004

**Left: Pynsent Cottage** in 2004

# THE GREEN

*Above:* **THE GREEN** 1927. **West End Stores** on the left and roadworkers caravans parked on The Green to the right of the picture.

*Above:* **THE GREEN (north side)** showing **Green Farm barns** and **West End Stores** in 1950, with schoolchildren maypole dancing on The Green in front of the crowned May Queen on her throne to the left of the picture

*Right:* **THE GREEN (north side).** Aerial photograph taken in the early 20th century showing **Green Farm**, **Pynsent Cottage** (at the left of the picture) and **West End Stores**. **Laurel House** (Chapel Lane) is at the middle right of the picture.

# THE GREEN

**Left and Below Right: West End Stores.** Two photographs, taken in the early 20th century, showing the property when it was Mrs Rose Harris' shop.

**Below: West End House** in 2004, now a private residence

**Above:** Detail of part of Chapel Lane showing **The Chapel** which was demolished in 1971

# THE GREEN

**Above: The Cottage,** Chapel Lane. This picture was taken in 1950. It has been substantially altered since then.

**Above: Laurel House,** Chapel Lane, is of early 17th century origin and for many years was the home and workshop of the Harding family, who carried on the business of builders and undertakers there from 1870 until 1970. It was later the home of a daughter of the family until 1991. This picture was taken in the mid 20th century.

**Right: Laurel House** on a snowy morning, December 1999

# THE GREEN

**BACK STREET** *(now The Green for postal purposes). In this picture looking towards the Top Green,* **The Lamb Inn** *is on the left and* **Green Acre** *and the terrace of cottages known as* **The Rank** *are on the right. The high wall to the extreme right no longer exists. The photograph was probably taken early in the 20th century at a time when no telephone or electricity cables spoilt the view.*

# THE GREEN

**Left: BACK STREET,** The Green from Chapel Lane to Green View. This photograph was probably taken in the early 1960s, before the house now called **Chapel House** was built, but not much earlier (note the number of TV aerials). The cottage on the right of the picture, now called **Anvil House**, was at one time a blacksmith's forge. **The Rank** cottages are on the left.

**Below Left: Green Acre** thought to be of 18th century origin. In the early part of the 20th century, when this picture was taken, the owners were agents of C & T Harris of Calne, and pork products, vegetables and sweets were sold from the little room to the right of the picture. The photograph shows Jehu (generally known as John) Willis, his wife Annie (nee Crook) and one of his eight children.

**Right: Green Acre** in 2000. The wisteria on the front of the house was removed in 2004.

# THE GREEN

*Above: **The Lamb Inn** c1920*

*Above: **The Lamb Inn** in 2004*

**Below: The Lamb Inn Garage**. *This was once a stable with hayloft above and is now the Urchfont Community Shop. The photograph was taken in 2004 before work on the shop had started.*

***Right: The Urchfont Community Shop and Post Office*** *2005.*
*This community shop developed, managed and staffed by local residents opened on Saturday 19 Feb 2005.*

# THE GREEN

***Left: Hales Farm.*** *These two farm cottages were built in 1895 and this photograph was probably taken about that time.*

***Right: Hales Farm*** *in 2004. The left-hand cottage is now called* **Crab Apple Cottage.**

**Below: Church Farm** *A view from the church tower taken in the mid-20th century with Church Farm in the centre and beyond that the orchard ground which was developed in the 1960s as The Orchard.* **Urchfont Manor** *can be seen in the far background.*

**Above: Church Farm House.** *A photograph taken in 1947 when the farm was part of the Urchfont Manor Estate sold at auction by the Executors of Mr Hamilton Rivers-Pollock, deceased. The oldest part of Church Farm House, on the left in this picture, probably dates from the 15th century when the house is believed to have been an open hall house.*

# THE GREEN

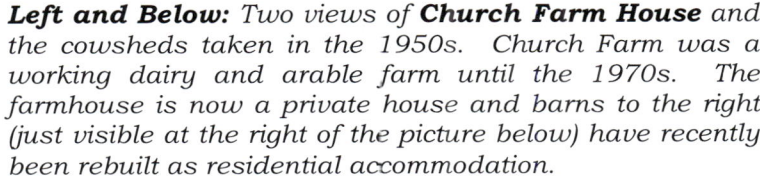

**Left and Below:** Two views of **Church Farm House** and the cowsheds taken in the 1950s. Church Farm was a working dairy and arable farm until the 1970s. The farmhouse is now a private house and barns to the right (just visible at the right of the picture below) have recently been rebuilt as residential accommodation.

**Left: Church Farm House** *in 2005*

# THE GREEN

**Left: Green View, Back Street**. *This picture probably dates from the first half of the 20th century, before mains water was supplied to the village in the 1950s. Note the well (see inset detail) at the front of the property. The 18th century cottage, formerly three cottages, was at that time the home of the village thatcher, Jesse Potter. The thatch was replaced with tiles in the 1970s after a fire destroyed the roof.*

**Right: Green View** *in 2000*

# Cuckoo Corner and Crookwood Lane

The area to the north of The Green up to and including Cuckoo Farm is Cuckoo Corner, formerly known as Cuckolds Corner. Crookwood Lane runs from Cuckoo Corner towards Potterne Wick.

***Cuckoo Farm*** *and* ***Breach Farm:*** *An aerial view taken in the mid-20th century when both were working farms*

# CUCKOO CORNER

**Above: Wayside Cottage** *2003. This little cottage is hidden away at the end of a narrow track between Breach House and the modern house called Cuckoo's Corner.*

**Urchfont CE (Controlled) Primary School.** **Left:** *A view taken of the front in 2000.*
**Right:** *Showing the new extension built in 2004.*

# CUCKOO CORNER

*Above: **Cuckoo Farm** in 1947 when the Urchfont Manor Estate was sold by auction (photograph from the Particulars of Sale). Later the farm became separated from the farmhouse and Cuckoo Farm became a private residence.*

*Above: **Breach Farm**, photographed in 1947, was also included in the Urchfont Manor Estate and sold by auction. This property was at that time a small farm where the splendidly named Wilfred Wagstaff Wildgoose, former landlord at The Lamb Inn, kept a herd of Jersey cows. The farmhouse is now a private house, re-named **Breach House**, with holiday cottages **(below)** where farm buildings once stood.*

*Left: **Cuckoo Farm** and '**The Farm Yard**' in 2004. One of the houses in The Farm Yard includes an interesting old barn with beamed roof, just visible on the right of this picture. The other properties in the development were built in 2004.*

# CUCKOO CORNER

**Left: Crookwood Farm** stands at the far north west of the parish on Crookwood Lane. The picture was probably taken in the mid-20th century.

**Crookwood Farm** in 2004

# Peppercombe and Church Lane

This area forms the northern boundary of the village, with the Village Hall providing an important focus for social life. The topography of the area with its steep sided combes and hangings is quite distinctive. The area was once part of the Northcombe Manor Estate.

**PEPPERCOMBE LANE.** *Aerial view taken in April 1966, with* **Church Farm** *(The Green) in the foreground and* **Yew Tree Cottage** *and* **Larchcombe** *towards the top of the picture. The redbrick building next to* **Yew Tree Cottage** *was later demolished and replaced with* **The Pump House***. The bungalow,* **Peppercombe***, is at the top right.* *(Courtesy Skyviews Aerial Archives)*

# PEPPERCOMBE

**Left: Peppercombe Mill** *1897, with the Miller, James Stone and his wife. The Mill was built around 1760 and was in use until early in the 20th century. It was demolished in 1911. Remains of the Mill (below in 2004) and the leat can still be seen.*

**Below Left: Willis' Cottage** *c1910, the home of Mr and Mrs Willis. Mrs Willis was the daughter of Mr and Mrs Wells who lived at the top of Peppercombe Lane in Peppercombe Cottage (see opposite page). Mr Wells installed a personal telephone line to connect the two cottages. Willis' Cottage was demolished in the early 1950s to make way for the building of the* **Sewage Works** *(below right in 2004). The new extension at the rear of the sewage works was built in 2002–3.*

PEPPERCOMBE

**Above: Larchcombe** and **Peppercombe Cottages** c1900. Larchcombe (on the left of the picture) was once the home of Dolly Lyne. The cottages (on the right) have since been demolished. Mr and Mrs Wells (see opposite page) lived in one of them.

**Above: Larchcombe** and **Peppercombe** bungalow in 2004

**Right: Yew Tree Cottage,** Peppercombe Lane c1918, with Jack and Beatrice Harris and their son Felix with Nurse Giddings. The house has been considerably extended in recent years and a conservatory added.

# PEPPERCOMBE

***Above Left: Urchfont Village Hall*** *in 1929, without the porch or the kitchen at the rear which were added later (see the picture taken in 1930, **above right**). The Village Hall was built by local residents on a voluntary basis, commemorated by a plaque over the front door. The spelling 'Erchfont' used on the plaque was then in common use.*

***Below: The Village Hall*** *in 2005 with side extension which was added in 1977*

***Above: Hardston****, Church Lane in the early 1950s. The Nissen hut in the front garden was used to house soldiers billeted in the village during the Second World War. **Hardston**, built in 1950, was the third bungalow to be built in Urchfont. The bungalow **Greystones** is on the right of the picture.*

# PEPPERCOMBE

**Left: Church Lane Cottages.** This row of cottages stood at the end of Church Lane, next to Thatched Cottage, where Gay Look now stands. They were declared to be scarcely fit for habitation in 1932 and were demolished in the mid-20th century. During the Second World War they were used by the Army for storage purposes. This picture must have been taken when, judging by the washing on the line, they were still inhabited.

**Right: Thatched Cottage**, Church Lane, a view from the church tower 2003. This brick cottage, built prior to 1730, has been whitewashed in recent years. It was at one time known as Emmie's Cottage, after Emmie Smith. **Gay Look** is on the left of the picture.

# THE CHURCH

***St Michael and All Angels Church*** *in 2005 with the War Memorial to the right of the picture*

# St Michael and All Angels

The church is the largest and oldest building in the village. The chancel arch c1220 is believed to be the oldest part of the original church still standing. The remaining part of the present building is mainly of 14th century origin with later additions. The tower and north aisle were built in the 15th century.

**St Michael and All Angels Church** (print) circa 1750.
*This is the earliest known picture of the church.*

# THE CHURCH

**St Michael and All Angels Church**
**Above:** Circa 1930    *(Courtesy CPRE)*

**Left:** Pictured in 1999 in the snow

**Upper Right:** The chancel with its vaulted interior at Christmas time.

**Right:** In 1924 showing the oil lamps used to light the church prior to electricity coming to Urchfont in the 1930s

# The Pond Area

Identified as early as 1784 on the Duke of Queensberry Map, Urchfont Pond remains a much admired and characteristic feature of the village to this day. Until the 1930s the Pond was an important part of the farming economy of the village providing water for cattle and horses. Today the Pond is home to ducks and fish. Visiting birds such as wagtails, herons, swallows and swifts enhance the scenic value of the heart of the village.

**Urchfont Pond** *2003*

# THE POND

**THE POND**

**Left:** Probably taken in the late 19th or early 20th century, this picture of the Pond shows **Mulberry House** in the middle and the **Church** in the background. An old crumbling wall and barn (since demolished) are on the right and a large beech tree is on the left.

**Right:** A picture taken in 1911 which shows the fenced off area to the right of the Pond where the cattle from Manor Farmyard used to drink. The tree to the right of Mulberry House has grown considerably since the earlier picture was taken, but the little tree in front of the house seems to have been lopped. On the right is the **Vicarage** and the rebuilt wall and barn of Manor Farmyard.

# THE POND

**Left: THE POND** 1911. *The first time in living memory that the Pond had dried up completely.*

*An unusual picture of* **THE POND** *looking from the opposite direction towards* **Friars Cottage** *on the left,* **Stanley House** *centre and* **Beechcroft** *(now Beech House) on the right*

**THE POND** *a later view, the large beech tree on the left has gone and the magnificent cedar tree is revealed*
(Courtesy CPRE)

# THE POND

**THE POND** *with a good view of the cedar tree and* **Mulberry House**. *The side of* **Church Cottage** *(since demolished) can be seen to the right of the picture.*

THE POND

**THE POND**. *A snowy scene, 1983.*

**THE POND**. *Thursday, 2nd January 2003, at 11:30 am after the collapse of the Great Lebanese Cedar tree due to a honey mould fungus in its roots. A very sad day but fortunately no one was hurt.*

# THE POND

*Left:* **Manor Farm House** rebuilt in the 18th century on the stone foundations of an earlier 16th or 17th century house that is thought to have been the Manor House before the present Urchfont Manor was built

*Below:* **Manor Farm House** in 2005, not much has changed apart from the front door

*Above:* **The Granary Barn, Manor Farm House** built in the early 19th century on staddle stones to prevent rat infestation.

*Right:* **Manor Farmyard** 2004

# THE POND

*Aerial view of* **THE POND** *and* **HIGH STREET**

# THE POND

**Left: Mulberry House** with the **Church** in the background. Originally two small cottages, perhaps dating back to the 16th century, Mulberry House was enlarged and re-fronted in the early 1700s. It takes its name from the old Mulberry tree in the back garden. It was for many years the home of the village Doctor who had his surgery there. *(Courtesy Wiltshire CC Libraries)*

**Right: Church Cottage** 1896. This was the verger's cottage and stood to the right of the church gate until it was demolished to make room for the new Rectory drive in the late 1960s. The picture shows the verger Mr Price and his family.

**Left: The Rectory** 2004, built in 1968-9 in the former kitchen garden of The Old Vicarage

THE POND

**The Vicarage**, *front view. The Vicarage is thought to have originated as a timber framed building, but was substantially altered and enlarged in the mid-19th century.*

**The Vicarage**, *back view, showing the extensive greenhouses which once stood in the garden*

**The Old Vicarage**, *front view 2004*

**The Old Vicarage**, *back view 2004*

# THE POND

*Aerial view looking towards **St Michael's Church** April 1966, with a good view of the **Vicarage** in the centre of the picture and, just above, the Vicarage stable block with coach house and hayloft which were demolished when the Rectory was built. **Church Cottage**, also demolished, is to the right of **Mulberry House**. **Manor Farm House** is at the bottom left of the picture and **Manor Farmyard**, then a working farm, is at the bottom right.* (Courtesy Skyviews Aerial Archives)

# THE POND

*Aerial view of the west side of **The Pond** April 1966 showing the chicken factory which closed in 1997*
*(Courtesy Skyviews Aerial Archives)*

**Cedar View** and **Rose Cottage** 2004, and to the right **Newbury House** and **Church Farm House**

**Beechcroft**, now renamed Beech House

# THE POND

**The Club House.** Originally two semi-detached cottages built c1750, it was rebuilt in 1800 following a fire and purchased in the 1870s by Wadworths Brewery for use as a Working Men's Club and Reading Room. It reverted to use as a private house in the 1920s and was the Post Office in the 1930s.

**Above: The Club House** when it was a Working Men's Club and Reading Room. On the left of the picture is **Newbury House** built in 1854, but believed to incorporate one or two earlier cottages. Beyond, in the middle of the picture, is **Church Farm House** (see The Green chapter).

**Right:** The same scene in 2004

# HIGH STREET

The High Street stretches from The Club House and Newbury House at its northern end to Sarum House and Hawthorns (at the foot of Stonepit Lane) at its southern end and includes for postal purposes The Rectory and the properties round the Pond. This area is the historical heart of the village and of the Conservation Area, with many of the properties listed as being of architectural and/or historical importance. The Pond itself (see previous chapter) is the focal point of the village for local residents and visitors alike where many of the community social and celebratory events are held.

*Aerial view of part of **HIGH STREET** from The School to the Pond and Church. 1930*

# HIGH STREET

**Left: White House** in the early 20th century. Built in the late 17th century, White House was once a cooper's (barrel maker's) shop. In the background on the left is **Oak Tree Cottage**.

**Below Left:** The same view taken in 2004

**Below: Oak Tree Cottage** in 2004

# HIGH STREET

*Aerial view of the former barn (since reconstructed and converted to* **Barn House**), **The Old Barn** *and the* **Butcher's Shop**, *April 1966*
(Courtesy Skyviews Aerial Archives)

**Below Left: Barn House** 2004. *Rear view of the reconstructed and converted former barn (shown to the left in the aerial view above) which had burnt down in August 1983.*

**Below: The Old Barn** 2004

# HIGH STREET

*Left:* **The Old Barn** and **Fuller's Saddlery** looking down the High Street to **Rowlands**. The pollarded ash known as the 'dumpty' or 'knobbly tree' standing at the road side was used to display saddlery items.

*Below:* The same premises later became the **Butcher's Shop**, pictured here in 1999 just before William Ford gave up the business.

*Inset:* The notice in the window indicating that Mr Ford would cease trading on 30th January 1999. The premises have since been converted into a private house.

*Below:* **Fuller's Saddlery**, probably taken in the 1920s when the business was moved over the road from its former premises at The Rockeries (see Townsend chapter)

HIGH STREET

***Above and Below Left: Eastville House*** *in the early 1900s. Eastville House was the first village Post Office, with the first telephone number 'Chirton 1'. It is now known as* ***Hanover House***. *The premises now known as* ***The Old Butcher's Shop*** *are on the left of the picture above.* ***Below Right:*** *The same premises 2004, both now converted into private houses.*

# HIGH STREET

***The Triangle, The Forge, The Garage and Hillsborough***, three pictures of the same area showing the changes of use over the years. The single storey building in the middle of these pictures was once the forge, later it was a bicycle shop and now is the garage for The Forge.

# HIGH STREET

*Right: **Urchfont House** 1904.*
Dating from the late 18th century with subsequent additions, Urchfont House (on the right) has two false windows at the front right-hand side (which may possibly have originally been real windows blocked off as a means to lessen the liability to window tax, but much more likely were simply painted on for the sake of symmetry). There is a substantial coach or carriage house to the right of the house. To the left of the picture is **The Rockeries**, then the saddler's business premises (see the Townsend chapter).

***Below Right: The Forge** 2004*

***Below: Urchfont House** and **The Rockeries,** 2004*

# HIGH STREET

**Left and Below Right: The Nags Head** late 19th century. Note that these pictures were taken before The Tiled House was built.

**Below Left: The Nags Head** with **The Forge** to the right of the picture, pictured when it was a Post Office run by Mr and Mrs Bill Cullimore

# HIGH STREET

***The Nags Head*** early 20th century, after ***The Tiled House*** was built and used as a shop. The picture **right** shows bread, cakes and groceries ready on the cart for delivery by Jack Harris (father of Felix) and Tom Long to customers in Urchfont, Wedhampton and Chirton. Charlie Stone, the owner of Stone's Bakery (see next page), is on the right of the picture.

***HIGH STREET*** 2004, as it is today festooned with overhead electricity cables

# HIGH STREET

**Above: Stone's Bakery** (now **Two Chimneys**) and beyond, to the left of the picture, the **Old School**

**Above: Stone's Bakery and Grocery Shop** 1924, showing Charlie Stone with his step-son, Ernie Pottenger, standing by the delivery van, and Harry Bratchell of Chirton. The business began in 1858 and remained with the Stone family until 1951. It continued as a general store run by Ned and Kath Smith until the 1970s.

**Left: (from left to right)** the 'dumpty' or 'knobbly tree', **Rowlands**, the **Old School** and **Stone's Bakery**

*Coronation celebrations in the* **HIGH STREET** *(looking towards* **Urchfont House***), June 1911*

# HIGH STREET

***The School*** *early 20th century, with children emerging from the school after classes*

***The Old School.*** **Left:** *Side view 2000.* **Right:** *Front view 2004.*
*Built in the early 19th century, the school building is now a private house.*

# HIGH STREET

**Below Right: Pear Tree Cottage** as it is now

**Below:** The former slaughterhouse, now a workshop, opposite Pear Tree Cottage pictured in the mid-1970s  (Courtesy WI)

**Left: Pear Tree Cottage** *1921 with thatched extension, and a side view* **right**, *with School Lane to the left. The cottage was once a butcher's shop owned by the Price family, who moved from Rowlands in the early part of the 20th century, and later by Mr 'Butcher' Smith and his wife (nee Price) until the mid-1950s. The cottage was known until recently as 'The Retreat'*

# HIGH STREET

***Above:*** **Rowlands**, early 20th century, before Mr Price opened his butcher's shop there. **Pear Tree Cottage** is in the centre of the picture and the **School** is on the extreme right. Note the gate into what is now St Michael's Close.
***Above Right:*** In 1910 with Mr Price and his family outside the shop extension.

**Rowlands**, probably in the 1940s, with Ernie Pottenger in the garden

**Rowlands** in 2003

# HIGH STREET

**Right: Inglefield** mid-1970s. Once a butcher's shop, it was part of the Watson-Taylor Erlestoke Estate until sold by auction in 1907 and later was a small farm. It is now in a state of disrepair. *(Courtesy WI)*

200

201

**Above: Slaughter House** 2004. This little building behind Inglefield was the slaughterhouse when Inglefield was a butcher's shop.

**Right: Inglefield Barn**, mid-1970s (since demolished) *(Courtesy WI)*

202

# HIGH STREET

***Above: The Tiled House*** *1924 when it was Bond's grocery shop (on the left of the picture) and **Rowlands** when it was the Post Office (on the right)*

***Above: The Tiled House*** *1911 when it was Glass's store and the Post Office. It was built c1904.*

***Right: The Tiled House, The Post Office*** *and **Wheelwrights** 2002*

# HIGH STREET

**Above: Friars Cottage** (middle) and **The Well House** (right) when it was a shop

**Above: The Well House** (left) and **The Old Bakery** (right), early 20th century

**Left: The Well House** and **The Old Bakery** in 2005, both now private residences

# HIGH STREET

***Friars Cottage.*** A late 16th/17th century timber framed cottage, it was once the Post Office and is reputed to have had the deepest well in the village, but this has now been filled in.

***Right:*** The side and back of **Friars Cottage**

***Below Right:*** The timber framed outbuilding in the garden with numbered timbers

***Below:*** Front view of **Friars Cottage**

# HIGH STREET

**Left: Wheelwrights** 2000. Formerly known as 'Shirley', this mid-18th century house was once a smallholding and became a blacksmith's shop in the mid-19th century. From the early 20th century it was the home and business premises of Bert Eves, the village wheelwright, and later his son, Lester, who carried on business there as carpenter and builder. Lester was the last wheelwright in the village. It is now a private house.

**Right: The Post Office** 2000. This 18th century house was the village Post Office for about 25 years before it closed in 2003. It is now a private house.

# HIGH STREET

**Stanley House** in 2002. It was requisitioned in the Second World War and used as an Officers' and Sergeants' Mess at different times.

**Stone's Yard** 2000. A poultry processing business was carried on here until 1995. At one time it dealt with 30,000 chickens a week.

**Oakston** 2004 (formerly Stone's Yard), one of two houses recently built on the poultry business site

# The Bottom

Formerly an area rather than a street name, 'The Bottom' is now generally used to refer to the road which was once divided into Friar's Lane, Ram Alley, The Ham, and Frog Alley as well as the Bottom itself. This was the 'East End' of the village and houses were generally smaller and poorer than those of the High Street and The Green – some of them being built into the greensand banks of this narrow valley.

**Bratchell's Cottage.** *This pair of cottages was out of use by the mid-1900s although the lower parts of their walls could be seen well into the 1990s. Though attractive in this picture, the ground is the lowest part of The Bottom and they are reputed to have been very damp.*

# THE BOTTOM

**Above: Bluebell Cottage** (formerly **Vale Cottage**). The house was extended whilst this book was in production.

**The Sawmills**. The picture (**above**) shows the sawmill itself and the adjoining cottage, which functioned as a pub – indicated by the bottle ends in the wall. These are two of the three cottages which are now one house known as The Sawmills, as shown (**below right**) in 2004.

**Below:** This picture shows the lane leading on behind the sawmills, including (on the right of the picture) a cottage since demolished.

THE BOTTOM

**Above: The Sawmills Yard** with logs and a haystack, at the foot of what is now The Ham

**Above: The Sawmills** (left), **Rivendell** (right) 2004, viewed from The Chute

**Right: Rivendell** on the left of the picture, adjoins The Sawmills. On the right are (from right to left) **Mountview Terrace** and a cottage since demolished, **Rockbourne Cottage**, **Grosvenor House** and **Revalle** (now called **Little Thatch**). The end of The Chute can also be seen.

# THE BOTTOM

*Left: **Grosvenor House**, the larger house in the centre of the picture, was built in 1893 to replace an earlier cottage in the same position. The two adjoining thatched cottages have been demolished, and Grosvenor House extended over their site. To either side, **Rockbourne Cottage** (right) and **Revalle** (now **Little Thatch**) (left) remain largely unaltered.*

*Below (left to right): **Yew Tree Cottage, The Cavern** and **Little Thatch**, all photographed in 2004, have changed little since they were built*

# THE BOTTOM

*These pictures of* **THE BOTTOM** *looking towards* **(right)** *and away from* **(below)** *the village, give some idea of what a crowded residential area this was in the late 19th century.*

**Hillview Cottage (right)** *now has an extension behind and a dormer in the thatch – and the hedge is much taller! On the other side of the road is the dipping well, once known by local schoolchildren as 'Jerusalem'. The thatched house at the end of the terrace on the left was demolished in the mid-1900s.*

**Below:** *The single cottage in the background has been much extended into* **1 & 2 Rose Cottages (below right)** *in the lane called The Baishe (pronounced 'Boysh')*

229

230

231

# THE BOTTOM

**Cranfield (above right)** in 2004 has been much altered and extended from the original pair of cottages **(above)**, although their position can be seen in the layout of the windows **(below)**

**Below: The Old Sewage Works,** looking towards The Bottom and the village from the bottom of Damson Chute. Built in the 1950s to serve the council estate at Crooks Piece, it was in use for only a few years before being demolished.

# UPHILL

Uphill remains an area of the village rather than merely a street, confusing visitors by including these cottages and an isolated bungalow as well as the road which bears the name.

**Uphill Cottages** (not to be confused with Uphill Cottage – see later) show few changes during the 20th century although windows have been enlarged. The 'mud house' in the background of the old picture **above left** (probably taken in the early 20th century) has been replaced by a modern bungalow.

# UPHILL

**Kit Hays** in the course of extension

The adjoining **Rookery Cottage**

**Kit Hays** and **Rookery Cottage** in 2004

**Left: Uphill Farm**, the farmhouse in 1889 and **right** in 2004. Although the pictures are very different, the house is in fact little altered, the earlier picture being taken from the garden and the modern one from the road.

**Above: Uphill Farm Pond** *(left) and* **Carina Cottage** *(right)*

**Below:** *The same view, showing the site of the pond now filled in.* **Carina Cottage**, *now one house, used to be two cottages, the right one being 'Carina' and the left one being named 'Ardgowan'.*

**Carina Cottage** 2004

**Gaddon House** 2004

# UPHILL

**Above: Firlings** and **Jasmine Cottage** are owned by a Trust set up by Mrs Sarah Gale in the 1970s for the benefit of long-standing local residents

**Franklin's Farm**. The older picture **(above)** shows a haystack in the yard. In the modern picture **(below)** taken in 2004 a recent extension can be seen.

**Below: Uphill Cottage** is much extended from the original building (shown on the right of the picture)

# Foxley and Crooks Lane

Only three houses survive at Foxley Corner, although the fact that one is number 9 suggests there were once at least six more. Crooks Lane once formed the eastern boundary of the village of Urchfont – until the council estate of Crooks Piece was built beyond it in the 1950s. The estate was redeveloped (and renamed Foxley Fields) in the 1990s.

**Crooks Piece.** The wider view *(left)* shows **Rookery Farm** at the lower left and **Uphill** in the top half of the picture, as well as the Crooks Piece estate to the right. The enlargement *(right)* gives a clearer view of Crooks Piece itself.

**Above:** Houses in **Crooks Piece**, newly built in the 1950s

Two more views looking into the former **Crooks Piece (above)** and modern **Foxley Fields (below)**

**Below:** The same view, now **Crooks Lane**, in 2004

**Rookery Farm House** pictured in 1938 (with John Snook as a young boy standing in the car)

Barn at **Rookery Farm House** 1938. This barn, since demolished, was at one time used to store mangles. On the back of this picture is written, 'Hatching Day April 1938'.

*Right: Rookery Farm House 2004*

# FOXLEY

*Above:* **Foxley Corner** 1904 looking eastwards from Urchfont village

*Above:* **Foxley Corner Cottage** and the same cottage **(below)** pictured in 2004 after the addition of a substantial extension

**Haydown** and **9 Foxley Corner** 2004

# Lydeway

This area astride the A342 derives its name, originally Lide Way, from the historic Devizes to Salisbury toll road and marks the watershed between the Bristol and the Christchurch Avon rivers. Much of the area was once part of the Urchfont Manor Estate and more recently the Heytesbury Hospital Estate.

**Bridge Cottage**, Lydeway 2004

**Sunnyside**, Lydeway 2004, was once the home of the Alexander family. Dick Alexander, one of the sons, used to farm at Franklin's Farm, Uphill.

# LYDEWAY

**Marsh Farm**, *Lydeway 2004, was once a cattle and horse infirmary owned by the Lancaster family, and is now owned by Richard Trowbridge and family*

**Dairy House**, *Lydeway April 1966. This house stood on the A342 on the other side of the road from nearby Marsh Lane and was demolished in the late 1960s. The remains of the fir trees in the front garden can still be seen.* (Courtesy Skyviews Aerial Archives)

**The Bell**, *Lydeway, was closed as a Wadworth's Inn in the late 1970s and is now a camping and caravan site. The Inn was used for a Coroner's Inquest in 1842. The thatched extension on the left and the central extension have been demolished.*

**The Bell**, *Lydeway 2004*

# LYDEWAY

**Above: Bellevue** (left) and **Little Thatch** (right), Lydeway 2004. Little Thatch was once a small farm with the adjacent field used for the Lydeway fete in the 1920s.

**Above Left: Lydeway Cottage** and **Garage** 1947, with Alexander's buses. Both properties together with the Bell Inn were once owned by Lawrence Alexander.

**Above Right: Lydeway Cottage** with Jim Nash and his wife. Once the site of a Police Station until the early 20th century, the cottage was demolished in the late 1960s and replaced by the present bungalow adjacent to the garage (**right**) photographed in 2004.

# LYDEWAY

**Above: Manor Farmhouse**, Lydeway 2004, in which three generations of the Plank family have lived. Part of the Heytesbury Estate until the late 1960s, the house was originally a small two-bedroomed thatched cottage. Some of the original thatch is still beneath the present roof tiles.

**Below: Andover House**, Lydeway 2004, was once the home of Stanley Alexander (brother of Lawrence), rabbit catcher on Salisbury Plain, and later of Ernie Pottenger who bequeathed Farmers Field to the Parish Council in 2000

**Left: The Old Potato Yard**, Lydeway 2004. The Yard and buildings are now used as a crafts centre, opened by the Rt Hon Michael Ancram M.P. in May 2001, where local crafts people make and sell their wares. In April 2003 a coffee/tea shop was introduced and in April 2004 a plant/bulb nursery was added.

# WEDHAMPTON – Street map

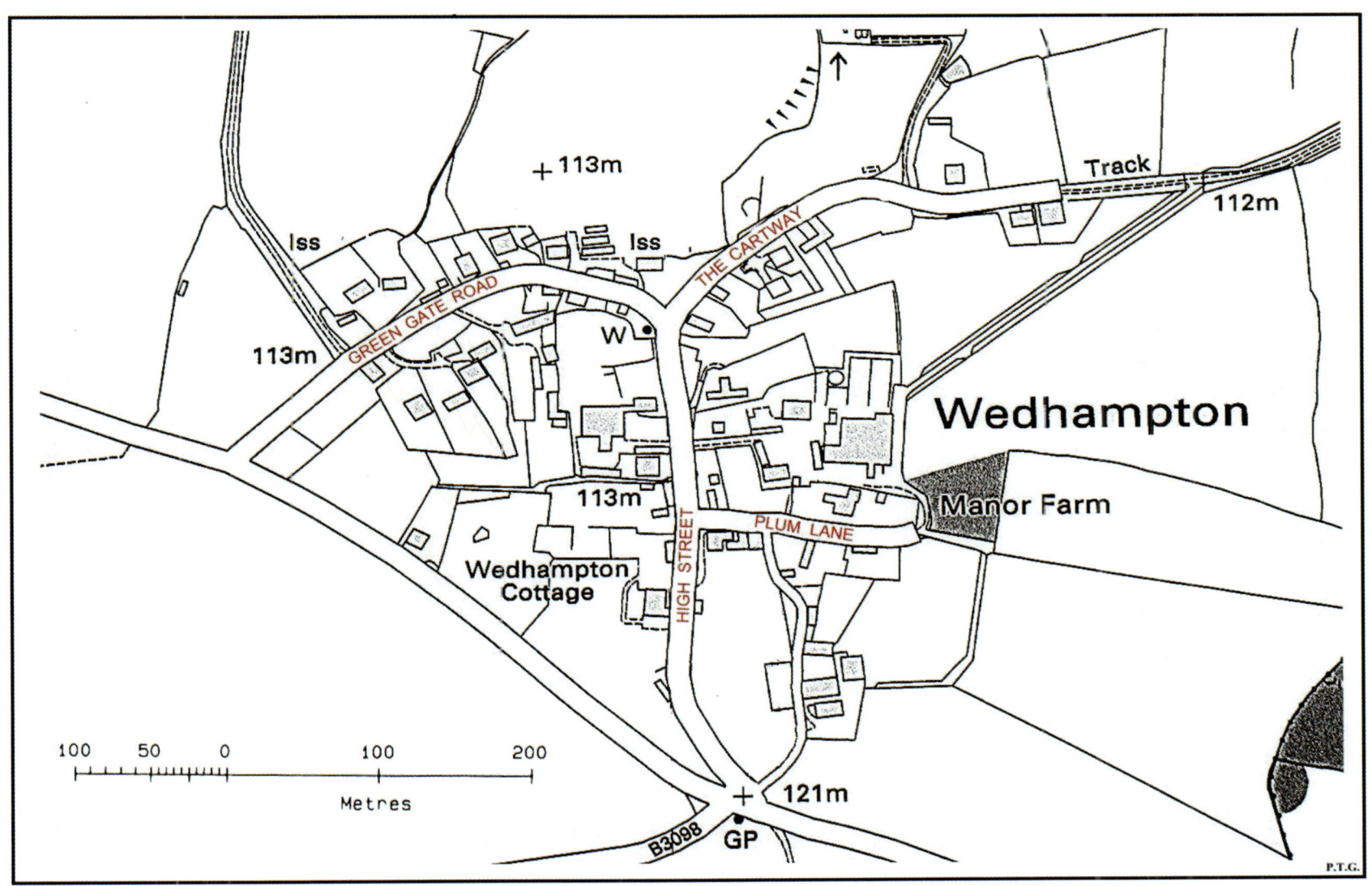

# WEDHAMPTON – Watson-Taylor Estate map 1832

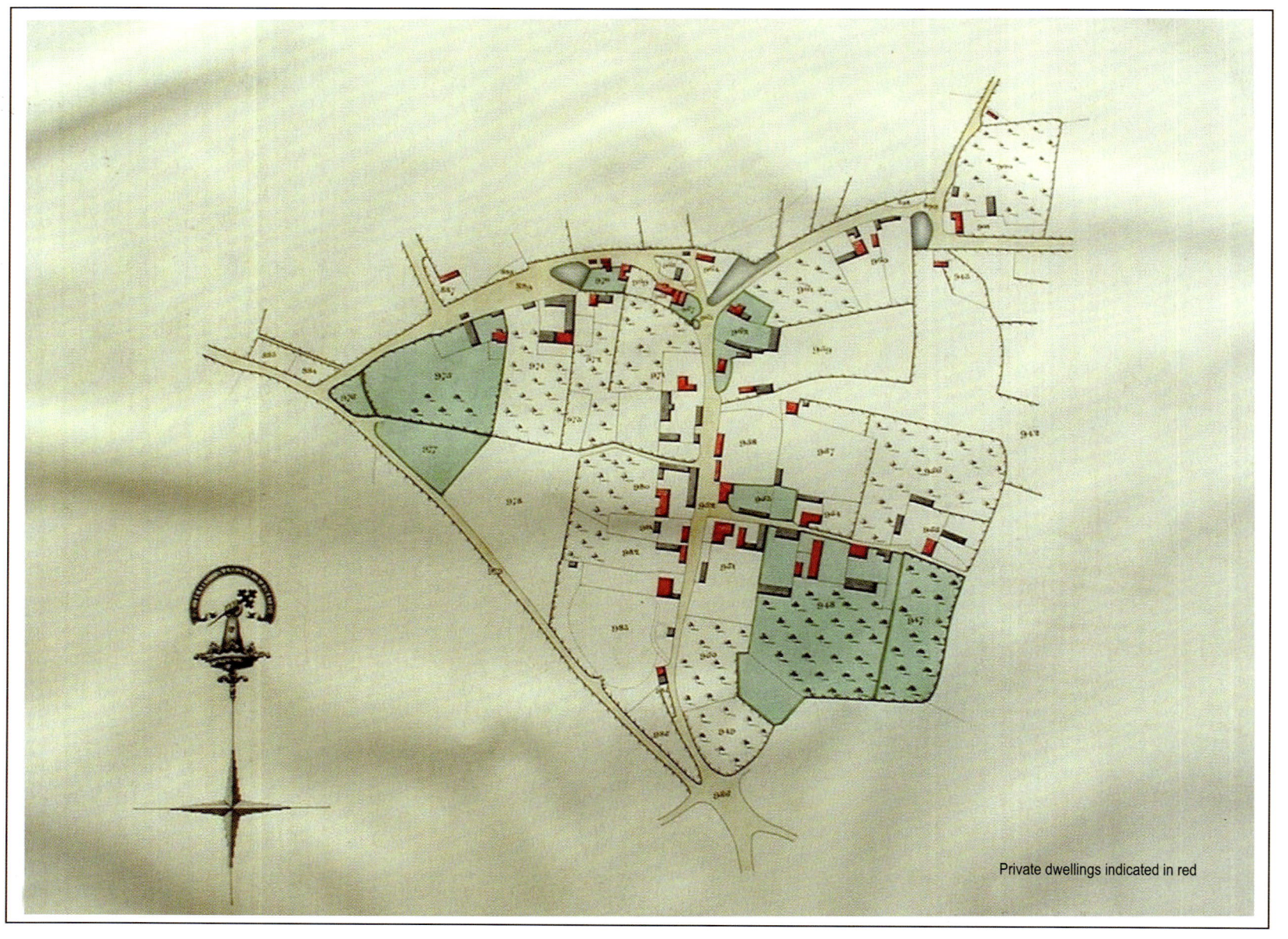

Private dwellings indicated in red

# Wedhampton

Whilst a separate community, and historically a distinct tithing, this village is an essential part of the civil parish of Urchfont and has in recent years shared some common land ownership through the Heytesbury Hospital Estate.

*Aerial view of* **WEDHAMPTON** *c1993    (Source Airpic)*

# GREEN GATE ROAD

**Left: GREEN GATE ROAD** *c1900. The western entrance to the village. The trees lining the road have all disappeared, but **Rose Cottage** can be seen on the left, and the bothy and **Windmill Cottage** in the centre. The ladies appear to be collecting horse manure for the garden.*

**Right: Lost Farmhouse (Langstone House site).** *Known only as 'Daddy Sligo's Farm', it was thatched and timbered and probably much the same age as Old Manor Farm (17th century). The building was demolished in the 1960s to make way for the development of Langstone House and Barham House.*

# GREEN GATE ROAD – WEDHAMPTON

*Left: **Rose Cottage** in 1975, largely as it was – a tied cottage, formerly lived in by William Drew, a farmworker. The small extension on the left was added in the 1950s by Leslie and Betty Waite.*
*(Courtesy Mrs M Woolfall)*

*Below: **Windmill Cottage** 1975. This cottage was built on common land in 1837 by John Edwards, a lime burner, together with a stable at the end of the garden.*
*(Courtesy Mrs M Woolfall)*

*Above: **Rose Cottage** 2004. The Cottage was extended to the left in the 1990s.*

# GREEN GATE ROAD – WEDHAMPTON

***Right: Fleece Cottage*** *1975. This stands on the site of earlier buildings that were incorporated into a staple barn when it was built in 1863 to grade and store wool fleeces; the date is in the brickwork on the facade. In the early 1900s the east end of the complex was converted back into a residence at a cost of £62! The modern west end of the complex was added in the 1990s.*
(Courtesy Mrs M Woolfall)

***Left: Fussell's Cottage****. A late 17th or early 18th century thatched and timber framed cottage. A former tenant was a Miss Fussell, hence the name.*

# GREEN GATE ROAD – WEDHAMPTON

**Left:** Junction of **GREEN GATE ROAD** and **HIGH STREET**
*An aerial view showing the cabbage patch where Cabbage Patch Cottage was built in the 1970s. To the right of the cabbage patch is **Spring Cottage** while opposite are **South** and **Vine Cottages** with **The Forge** to the right.*

**Right: Spring, South** and **Vine Cottages**
*1975 viewed from the centre of the village looking into Green Gate Road. Spring Cottage (left) was originally built as two thatched cottages and was later developed into one house. It was named after the well which is at the bottom left of the picture. South and Vine Cottages to the right are of 19th century origin and were formerly three cottages. South Cottage housed the Post Office opened in about 1936 but since closed.*
(Courtesy Mrs M Woolfall)

# The Cartway

**Above: The Old Chapel** as it was in the mid-20th century and **(right)** in 1975   *(Courtesy Mrs M Woolfall)*

The Chapel was built in 1867 as a Wesleyan Methodist meeting place and was closed in about 1964. In 1969 it was converted into a private house.

**Right: The Old Chapel** in 2004

# THE CARTWAY – WEDHAMPTON

***Left: Rybury Cottage and 17/18 The Cartway** 1975* showing the rear of Rybury Cottage and, to the right, 17/18 The Cartway. The latter were once three cottages. Rybury Cottage was always a single house and its garden had a large pond, since filled in.
(Courtesy Mrs M Woolfall)

**Right:** These two quite primitive cottages, dark inside, once stood to the side of Rybury Cottage. They were demolished to make way for the garage at Rybury Cottage.

**Below: Mount Pleasant Cottage.** This view is from the rear of these two cottages looking towards the Plain. They were demolished after the Second World War and replaced with two modern bungalows, one of which (**right**) has retained the name 'Mount Pleasant'. The last residents of the old Mount Pleasant Cottage were the grandparents of Mrs Evelyn Durrant who now lives in Vine Cottage.

***Below: Mount Pleasant** 2004*

# HIGH STREET

**Right: The Forge** 1975 an early 18th century thatched and rendered building, once the busy village forge  (Courtesy Mrs M Woolfall)

**Below: Lydgate Farmhouse** 1975. Originally a farmhouse that was extended in the 19th century but has changed little since the 1900s, with farm buildings and holdings in The Cartway. Evidence of an elaborate arched doorway and courtyard on the northern side was found during recent restoration work. The attached barn is now an Art Research Centre.  (Courtesy Mrs M Woolfall)

**Above: 22/23 High Street** 1975. Once one house but now two, it is thought to have been a bakehouse. No. 23 has a circular oven on the right of the inglenook fireplace and a very large smoke room above the inglenook.
(Courtesy Mrs M Woolfall)

# HIGH STREET – WEDHAMPTON

**Left:** Aerial view of **Old Manor Farm**. The farmyard was the site of the Wedhampton fire of 1883, started by a boy playing with 'lucifers', that resulted in the destruction of a farmhouse, two cottages just below **Timbers** (which is just visible at the top of the picture) and several barns. The farmhouse and cottages were demolished and not replaced. Only the thatch of Old Manor Farm itself was damaged. The barn/grain dryer at the top, opposite Timbers, was converted to a house, **The Barn**, in the 1970s.

**Old Manor Farm** 1929. A timber framed house of early 17th century origin enlarged by the addition of a wing later in the century. Once known as 'Uncle's Farm', the farmyard was the centre of the disastrous fire of 1883 (above).

**Above:** **Old Manor Farm** 2004 and, **left**, a detail of a wall of the barn with the name of the owner and, presumably, the date the barn was built. Forebears of the Ernle Drax family had owned land in Wedhampton from the 14th century.

# HIGH STREET – WEDHAMPTON

*Left:* **Timbers** front view and **(below)** the rear, photographed in 1975 after restoration in 1973. One of the oldest houses in Wedhampton, **Timbers** is a late 16th to early 17th century timber framed building with an oriel window in the front gable. A line of leylandii trees now hide the front of the house from view.  (Courtesy Mrs M Woolfall)

*Below Right:* **Wedhampton Manor Lodge** 2004, originally the gardener's cottage to the Manor, the lodge was extended to the right in the 1960s

*Below:* **Wedhampton Manor** 2004. Dating from about 1650, the Manor was enlarged and re-fronted in the latter part of the 17th century. The date 1701 and the letters 'HE & SE' (the initials of Henry Eyre and his second wife Susanna) can be seen on the rain water head at the north west corner of the building.

# HIGH STREET – WEDHAMPTON

*Left: An aerial view taken in April 1966 showing **Wedhampton Cottage** in the foreground and **Timbers** and **Wedhampton Manor** at the top of the picture*  (Courtesy Skyviews Aerial Archives)

*Below: **Wedhampton Cottage** in 1975. Probably of 17th century origin, the house was enlarged during the 19th century in the 'cottage ornée' style with an open veranda and three-light pointed arched dormer windows.*
(Courtesy Mrs M Woolfall)

*Below: **Wedhampton Cottage Stables** and **Coach House**, now a self-contained house to the left of the archway and a flat to the right. Further to the right in this picture is **Spring End**, which was formerly two dwellings and is now combined into one.*

# HIGH STREET – WEDHAMPTON

307

***Left: The Lodge** 1975. A view of the lodge cottage for Wedhampton Cottage showing the driveway off the High Street to the front of the big house. A bell on the lodge wall summoned the lodge-keeper to open the gates. The bell was still there until about 2000 when it was stolen.*
*(Courtesy Mrs M Woolfall)*

***Below: Chestnut Cottage (on the A342)** 2004. A former dairy cottage to Wedhampton Cottage built about the same time as the extension to the main house in the same 'cottage ornée' style. The extension to the right of the gable is modern.*

***Below: The Lodge** 2004, now fully restored and extended, and separated from Wedhampton Cottage by a wall and shrubbery*

308

309

# Plum Lane

*Right: **Old Manor Farmhouse** 2004. A 17th century thatched and timbered farmhouse.*

*Left: **Walnut Cottage** 1975. Once a building of importance as one house, it was subsequently divided into two cottages as shown here. Now fully restored it is one house again. The rear of Old Manor Farmhouse can be seen in the background.  (Courtesy Mrs M Woolfall)*

# PLUM LANE – WEDHAMPTON

**Left: Wyndhams House** *1975, built in the 19th century as part of the Wedhampton Manor Estate. It was significantly extended in the early 1980s and a new access made at the end of Plum Lane. The driveway shown in this picture is now part of the garden.*   (Courtesy Mrs M Woolfall)

**Below:** *The present front of the house with the porch removed from its original position. The small thatched building in the front can be seen to the right of the earlier picture above.*

**Above:** *In 2004, now called* **Wyndhams Farm House***, showing how the house has been extended to the left and the original driveway incorporated into the garden*

## OTHER URCHFONT PUBLICATIONS

*Urchfont by any other name*, 2001, ISBN 0-9540851-0-8
*Walks around Urchfont and Wedhampton*, 2001
*Urchfont and Wedhampton Heritage Maps*, 2000
*Urchfont Manor – The Evolution of a House and a College*, by Tom Barklem, 1977
*Welcome to Urchfont*, 2004

## AERIAL PHOTOGRAPHS

Some of the aerial photographs in this book have been reproduced with the permission of Skyviews Aerial Archives who hold the copyright. Reproductions of these photographs may be purchased in a display frame from Skyviews Aerial Archives, 17/18a Armley Park Court, Stanningley Road, Leeds, LS12 2AE (Telephone 0113-2794411).

## PRINTS

Apart from those pictures which are subject to copyright, reproductions of pictures contained in this book may be purchased on application to Urchfont Parish Trust.

## URCHFONT – SPELLING

Reference is made to the considerable number of spellings of 'Urchfont' in *Urchfont by any other name*. In this publication, the spelling 'Urchfont' is used throughout, regardless of the age or source of the photograph.